PANESE
ESTYLES

Gentle Nature and the Changing Se
At the Heart of Japanese Lifestyles

The Japanese archipelago lies off the eastern coast of Asia and face
two bodies of water, the Sea of Japan and the Pacific Ocean. Fou
large islands, Hokkaido, Honshu, Shikoku and Kyushu, stand ou
among many others, some large, most small. The narrow islan
chain, shaped like a bow, is oriented generally north-south.
This geographical layout has created temperature zones which ar
surprisingly different, considering the small area of the countr
Much of Japan is temperate, but the north (Hokkaido) is subarcti
while the south (Okinawa) is subtropical. Humidity varies great
too. Land facing the Sea of Japan has high humidity in winter, whi
the Pacific seaboard has it in summer.
These local climate differences are greatly responsible for the wid
diversity seen in each region's culture and way of life. Climate an
the four relatively distinct seasons have greatly influenced Japanes
culture. Japan is not the only country with four seasons, of cours
but the Japanese have always been keen, throughout their long his
ory, to regard the current season as a part of their lives. They d
his by expressing their emotions about current weather patterns
gladly adapting to the time of year, and simply enjoying what eac
season brings. This outlook forms the basis of Japanese cultur
and customs, and influences lifestyles today, even in the midst c
echnological improvements and Westernization.

40°

30°

CONTENTS

花
Flowers

鳥
Birds

風
Wind

月
Moon

「花鳥風月」

Translated literally, *ka cho fu getsu* means "flowers, birds, wind and the moon." This Japanese expression indicates love of the natural world around us.

CLOTHING

In Japan, the four seasons are quite distinctive, so clothing requirements for each season vary widely, with type of material, color and style being the main considerations. Everyday clothes are practically the same as those worn in North America and Europe. The demands of modern everyday life give little opportunity to wear the traditional kimono. However, it is still regularly seen at weddings, funerals and other ceremonies.

Consumers have a wide variety of clothing to choose from — items made in Japan, luxury brands from Europe and the U.S., and relatively inexpensive clothes from other Asian countries. Buying decisions depend on personal budgets and purpose.

Fashion magazines and other sources influence consumers, and purchases can be made through numerous channels, including catalogs. Some manufacturers produce small exclusive lots of clothing, thus targeting a specific type of customer. Overall, the clothing market is geared to satisfy all types of consumers.

▌Breakdown of Average Monthly Living Expenditures per Household (All Household Base)

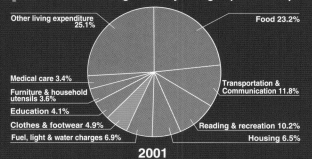

Other living expenditure 25.1%

Food 23.2%

Medical care 3.4%

Furniture & household utensils 3.6%

Education 4.1%

Transportation & Communication 11.8%

Clothes & footwear 4.9%

Fuel, light & water charges 6.9%

Reading & recreation 10.2%

Housing 6.5%

2001

Source: "Monthly Statistics of Japan", Statistics Bureau, Ministry of Public Management, Home Affairs, Post and Telecommunications

Change of Average Monthly Expenditures for Clothes & Footwear and Share in Living Expenditures per Household

	¥	%
1997	19,336	5.8
1998	18,013	5.5
1999	17,565	5.4
2000	16,188	5.1
2001	15,170	4.9

Spring and Summer
Clothing Basics

When the Weather is Unpredictable or Hot and Muggy, Casual Wear Is In.

At the beginning of spring the weather can be quite fickle, with some days warm and others cold. There can even be great differences during the same day, with morning and evening temperatures much cooler than those at mid-day. At such a time, it is a good idea to take a light garment — perhaps a sweater, cardigan or jacket — to wear over other clothes.

When the summer heat hits in July and August, day-time temperatures can often rise to the mid 30s (Celsius) throughout the country, with areas facing the Pacific Ocean particularly susceptible to high humidity levels. Casual clothes that "breathe" will help you get through those hot and muggy days. A T-shirt, informal shirt, or short-sleeved pullover shirt can be complemented by cotton pants, jeans or a casual skirt. Teenagers and young adults often prefer a T-shirt and have a wide choice, from famous sports brands to something inexpensive. The short-sleeved pullover shirt is a favorite among every age group, and well-known fashionable brands enjoy considerable demand every summer.

1

2

3

1. Cotton and short-sleeved pullover shirts are worn by young and old alike.
2. Children in shorts and short-sleeved shirts.
3. Young people like the casual look of T-shirts.
4. Ginza in Tokyo is one of Japan's most fashionable shopping districts.
5. This young girl has just started elementary school. Her red knapsack is an essential part of school life.
6. Harajuku is a fashionable mecca for the young in Tokyo.

Fall and Winter
Clothing Basics

When Cold Grips the Country, Practical and Trendy Coats Abound

Just as spring ushers in fickle weather, fall too cannot make up its mind. Clothing choices reflect those temperature fluctuations. When winter arrives in earnest around December, the mercury drops throughout the country, especially in Hokkaido where temperatures remain below freezing day after day. That is why, with the exception of Okinawa and other southerly regions, we need sturdy clothing to protect us from the cold. Today's homes, workplaces, trains, buses and stores are fully heated, so people prefer outer layers of clothing that can be put on and removed easily. Some common examples are sweaters and heavy casual shirts and, on top of these, coats and jackets. Materials are likely to be cotton, polyester, wool or leather, depending on the purpose of the clothing and the design desired. Colors for men tend to be monotone shades — perhaps a brown or navy blue — but women have a far greater choice in color and sometimes wear vibrant shades. Boots have become increasingly popular over the last few years, especially among adolescent and young adult women.

Average Monthly Clothing Expenditures per Household
(¥)

	1997	1998	1999	2000	2001
Total	19,336	18,013	17,565	16,188	15,170
Japanese - style clothing	880	764	697	669	600
Western - style clothing	7,746	7,064	6,916	6,284	5,971
Shirts and sweaters	3,724	3,617	3,533	3,281	3,047
Underwear	1,653	1,605	1,555	1,480	1,348
Others	5,333	4,963	4,864	4,474	4,204

Source: Statictics Bureau, Ministry of Public Management, Home Affairs, Post and Telecommunications

1. Enjoying life in Hibiya Park, Tokyo.
2. The *cha-baori* was a jaket used by practitioners of the tea ceremony, but is now worn over a cotton *yukata*. *Cha-baori* are commonly seen in Japanese inns.
3. Temperatures fluctuate considerably in the fall, so it's a good idea to take a light coat or jacket when you go out.
4. Children find denim jackets stylish.
5. Young people in duffel coats.
6. When doing the housework and other chores, older women often protect their clothes with this apron-like garment called a *kappogi*.

Uniforms

Today's Uniforms for Work and School Reveal Variety

A businessman will almost invariably wear a gray, brown or navy blue suit and a necktie when at work or traveling, although this is hardly a compulsory uniform. A businesswoman has relatively greater leeway in choosing her outfit, from a suit to something more casual. Her choices will depend on the type of business she is in. Female office workers generally must wear a uniform during working hours, regardless of the size of the company. Navy blue and other conservative colors give the appearance of neatness and efficiency, so these are favored.

Factory workers, technicians, laborers in the transport and retail industries, and store clerks customarily wear work clothes, regardless of their sex.

Many schools also insist on uniforms, one for summer and one for winter. Uniforms for junior and senior high school students throughout the country tend to adopt the same type of design — high collared jackets for boys, "sailor" suits for girls. An increasing number of private schools in urban areas have their students wear blazers. Rules for elementary children depend on the region, with some insisting on a uniform and others not. In many elementary schools, students wear uniforms during physical education classes.

1. Kids on their way home from elementary school. Children may be required to wear yellow hats when walking to and from school, so that drivers can see them more easily.
2. The uniforms of junior high school boys have high collars.
3. Senior high school girls in uniform. "Loose socks" are fashionable these days.
4. Female staff at a department store wear uniforms to emphasize their neatness and efficiency.
5. It is common for a factory or construction worker to wear a uniform or workman's outfit on the job.
6. A suit is a must for businesspeople and many female office workers. Monotones, often a variety of navy blue, are favored.
7. The type of uniform worn by female police officers in summer.

7

6

Fashion Trends

Famous Overseas Brands Enjoy Continuing Popularity in the Ever-Changing World of Fashion

Ever since Japan's economic bubble broke in the early 1990s, there has been a growing demand for cheap, quality clothes. One thing that has not changed, though, is the variability of fashion styles, with consumers displaying a wide assortment of preferences. One of the ways manufacturers gather information on this fickle market is by opening a few shops to test the waters. Then they develop clothes that accurately reflect preferred trends.

Against this backdrop, famous European and American brands still continue to be popular, especially among women, and a wide selection of clothes, bags, shoes and other fashion goods are available. Famous overseas brand items may be sold in stores owned by the companies themselves, consigned to agent stores, or sold through catalogue sales. The expansion in marketing channels has made shopping easy, and the latest foreign items hit the Japanese market almost as soon as they are seen on their home market.

Increasingly, clothes are being made out of recycled materials. One example is "fleece," which is made of recycled wool or even plastic bottles. At a time when consumers are showing greater interest in buying environmentally friendly clothes, manufacturers are keeping pace by developing "green" techniques to make them. More goods made of recycled products are appearing on the market, although companies still find it hard to make a profit in this area.

1

2

1. Tokyo Fashion Week is a show for fashion lovers in Japan.
2. These days, winter wear tends to favor duffel coats for both sexes, and boots with somewhat high heels for the ladies.
3. This "fleece," which is actually a recycled material made from plastic (polyethylene terephthalate) bottles, has recently become quite popular among outdoor enthusiasts.
4. Department stores sell a wide array of shoes for women. Famous overseas brands continue to attract many customers.
5. Magazines for the fashion conscious. Publishers tend to aim for a specific age group. Quite a few magazines are Japanese-language versions of foreign publications.
6. Takeshita Street in the Harajuku district of Tokyo has boutiques and small variety stores which appeal to the young crowd.

Mail Order/Direct Marketing Sales Ratio by Good & Services (FY2000)

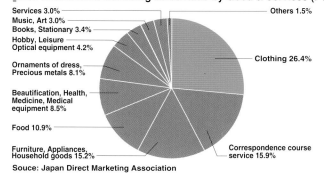

Services 3.0%
Music, Art 3.0%
Books, Stationary 3.4%
Hobby, Leisure
Optical equipment 4.2%

Ornaments of dress,
Precious metals 8.1%

Beautification, Health,
Medicine, Medical
equipment 8.5%

Food 10.9%

Furniture, Appliances,
Household goods 15.2%

Others 1.5%

Clothing 26.4%

Correspondence course
service 15.9%

Souce: Japan Direct Marketing Association

3

4

5

6

Traditional Attire

The *Kimono* Enhances Special Occasions

Whenever we think about Japanese traditional clothing, the first thing that springs to mind is the *kimono*. There are many types of *kimono*, depending on the age of the wearer, the occasion and the season. (See the article on *kimono*.)

Unfortunately, modern living in Japan affords very few opportunities to wear a *kimono*. Only a very small percentage of elderly women wear it on outings or when relaxing at home.

On the other hand, traditional clothing for women is still common at weddings, funerals and other events of a religious or social nature. For example, students wear a *hakama* at their graduation ceremonies, and women may wear a cotton *yukata* during summer festivities. Young women are apt to wear a colorful *kimono* to Coming of Age ceremonies, and many women also wear a *kimono* to shrines on New Year's Day. On these occasions, young people have a number of incentives for wearing traditional attire – to find out more about clothing unique to Japanese culture, to heighten the feeling of a "special" day, and to bestow upon the event a stronger impression for future memories.

The *kimono* embodies many aspects of Japanese aesthetic culture, notably ancient practices of weaving, sewing and embroidery. Recently, these traditional methods have been given a modern touch and western style, while still using the materials and sewing techniques seen in the traditional *kimono*. Thus, in some cases, the unique and aesthetic aspects of the *kimono* are being adapted to suit current sensibilities.

1. Parents and children dressed in *yukata*, playing with sparklers on a summer evening.
2. Young women called *maiko* entertain guests the traditional way at exclusive restaurants.
3. Women in *kimono*.
4. A wedding is a good place to see Japanese traditional clothes.
5. Parents visit a shrine with their newborn children to celebrate their birth and pray for their success and happiness.
6. *Tango no sekku*, the Boy's Festival, is held on May 5 to celebrate boyhood and ask the gods for good luck throughout life.
7. Girls in long-sleeved *kimono* enjoying the *Shichi-go-san* (7-5-3) Festival. The festival, held at shrines on November 15 to pray for special favors for children, is for 3- and 5-year old boys and 3- and 7-year old girls.
8. Students in *hakama* at their graduating ceremony. This formal wear closely follows Japanese tradition, except for the boots.
9. Taking a commemorative photo is an essential part of any graduation ceremony. More women are now wearing feminine suits to such occasions, rather than a *kimono* or *hakama*.

5

6

7

8

9

Unwavering Respect for Traditional Apparel
~ *Kimono* ~

The traditional *kimono* is well known and admired by Japanese of all ages, and by people of other nations as well.

Experts tell us that the *kimono*'s roots go back as far as the Jomon period, which began about 12,000 years ago. The clothing of those days was not as comfortable as the *kimono* of today, but a piece of cloth sewn into a cylindrical shape, with holes, somewhat like a dress. In the Heian period (794-1191), aristocratic women wore the *juni-hitoe*, a collection of about 12 layers of *kimono*-like garments, while commoners wore a far simpler garment tied with a thin belt of cloth. Then, during the Edo period (1603-1867), people became more fastidious about ways to tie the *obi* sash and arrange the hair and accessories. It was around this time that *Nishijin* woven silk fabrics and *Yuzen* dyeing methods became famous.

It is said that there are now nine types of traditional apparel. Five of the more common ones are *furisode*, *tomesode*, *homon-gi*, *hakama* and *yukata*. In the West, the choice of formal or semi-formal clothes depends on the time, place and occasion. This is also true for the *kimono*, but other conditions, particularly age and marital status, apply as well.

Furisode and *Tomesode* Kimono

The design of the long-sleeved *kimono* (*furisode*) has a connection with superstition. Since ancient times, the Japanese have believed that human life follows cycles, and that each cycle include an unlucky year, called *yakudoshi*. People expect to encounter two or three *yakudoshi* in a lifetime. A person's bad luck is said to even rub off on relatives and friends, so during their *yakudoshi* they may feel the need to take extra care. During New Year festivities, shrines and temples post notices listing the birth years and zodiacs of people who are entering a *yakudoshi* (men and women have different unlucky cycles). These religious institutions offer ways to avoid the bad luck. The extent to which these warnings are taken varies.

The long sleeves of the *furisode kimono* are supposed to sweep away bad luck. Girls are said to enter a *yakudoshi* at the age of 19, so many 20-year old women wear a *furisode kimono* when celebrating Adults' Day, symbolizing their desire to avoid bad luck. Even today, the *furisode kimono* is a mark of youthful femininity.

Incidentally, the long sleeves, because of their tendency to wave "suggestively," were also supposed to be able to attract the affections of a desired young man. The long-sleeved *kimono* therefore became the formal wear of young unmarried women. When she married, the new bride would cut her sleeves, making the *kimono* into a formal *tomesode* garment.

Homon-gi Kimono

The *homon-gi* ("for visiting") *kimono* is worn irrespective of age or marital status. It is often seen at tea ceremonies and formal parties, and is worn by some mothers at ceremonies marking their children's admission to a school. The name comes from the fact that this type of *kimono* was, until fairly recently, worn when visiting. Some *homon-gi kimono* have a pattern adorning the entire garment, while others have an artistic design — practically a picture — that begins at the bottom hem, spreads from there to the left shoulder, and ends at the collar. The "picture" even extends to the inside left sleeve.

A street scene in Kyoto

Hakama

Hakama are loose, wide-legged trousers. For a man, the formal effect is completed with a *haori* jacket on which a *mon* (family crest) appears. In ancient times, aristocratic women wore a type of *hakama* as an undergarment, and by the middle of the Heian period it had become outer wear. During the Meiji period (1868-1912), ladies at the Imperial Court were wearing *hakama* as a uniform and ceremonial garment. In time, girls began wearing them to school. Interest in this traditional wear is quite strong even today — at a graduation ceremony you will see some women in *furisode kimono*, others in *hakama*.

Women wearing *hakama* and long-sleeved *kimono*

Yukata

The casual *yukata* looks something like a *kimono*, but unlike the latter it is made of cotton and worn without a wrap-around undergarment. It is therefore ideal for summer wear, and quite commonly worn. You will see *yukata* on summer evenings, both at fireworks displays and on excursions in search of cool refreshing air. In Japanese inns and hotels, both men and women wear *yukata* as sleeping wear. *Yukata* are "in" now, and even one foreign clothing manufacturer has begun selling them.

It must be admitted that traditional Japanese clothes are not cheap. That is why they are passed from mother to daughter, father to son. In about 1982, it had become obvious that traditional apparel was being abandoned for cheaper, easy-to-wear, practical Western clothes. The *kimono* experienced a very slight upturn in 1989 and 1990, then fell into a serious slump again. (Information from *Gyoshubetsu Kashidashi Shinsa Jiten*).

Yet many young people still say they want to wear Japanese apparel at one time or another. In a survey conducted by the Nishijin Textile Industrial Association, more than 60% of all respondents (640 female university students in Kyoto, 1993) stated that they wanted to wear a *kimono* to a shrine or temple at New Year's, their Coming of Age ceremony, weddings and other formal occasions. In addition, a relatively impressive percentage (more than 5%) said they would like to wear one even on outings, dates and everyday occasions.

As times change, clothing preferences have veered decidedly toward practical Western clothing. Yet the inherent desire of the Japanese to preserve their culture has not changed. This affection for past traditions will surely remain strong in the 21st century.

Kimono pattern

Changing Japan, Changing Millennia

Changes in Japan's Consumer Market — The Three Generations

We can, I think, divide Japan's post-war consumer society into three different groups, each group representing a different generation. The first group is the war generation — people who experienced World War II. The second is the catch-up generation — people who typically reached adulthood in about 1965, and who helped Japan catch up with other industrialized nations. The third group is the "new breed" generation — people who became adults around 1985. As consumers, these three generations are completely different.

Members of the catch-up generation enjoy an affluent lifestyle symbolized by durable consumer goods, such as the 3 C's — cars, coolers (air conditioners) and color TVs. People of this generation are now in managerial positions. They helped Japan achieve high economic growth, and successfully weathered the so-called oil shock when oil prices rose sharply in the 1970s. The catch-up generation has two things in common with the older, war generation. First of all, both groups worked hard to achieve their goals. Secondly, men and women in both groups used to have different roles in society, the women spending a lot of time to buy things for the home, and the men working long hours for a company. The typical consumer trend in the catch-up generation is that they have a piano, a brand of whisky and drives a car that is "suited" with the position at the company.

Members of the new breed generation of consumers do not fit these descriptions. Their values are different, so their consumption patterns are different too. For example, women in the new breed generation are likely to be active outside the home. This gives them a degree of economic independence, but not much time to shop in a leisurely fashion. Another difference between the new breed generation and the catch-up generation is the way they look at foreign cultures. Members of the catch-up generation greatly admire certain aspects of foreign culture, but at the same time, has psychological complexes which lead to feelings of wariness. People in the new breed generation have no such complexes, so they tend to adopt many aspects of foreign culture without any difficulty. They happened to gain consumer clout at the same time pressures from outside Japan were pushing up the value of the yen to unprecedented levels. This exterior pressure coincided with pressures from within, as the new breed of Japanese consumers gained buying power. The result was a massive change in consumer patterns in Japan. This change is not perhaps readily apparent to the Japanese themselves, but it was significant enough to set in motion important changes within the country.

Trade Friction Between Japan and the U.S.A. — Japan Is Not Unique

One similarity shared by Japanese and American people is that they are both interested in new things and ideas. As a country, Japan is much older than the U.S., but people in the Japan of today have feelings and sensations which are far from old. Americans and Japanese like change, as is evident by the fact that American English and the Japanese language both keep changing. Both countries now have basically the same income levels, and their economies are growing at about the same rate. Post-war global consumption has been driven mainly by two countries, Japan and the U.S. But in spite of Japan's economic prowess, Americans tend to think of Japan as still trying to catch up to the U.S. And Japan's catch-up generation still believes that Japan and Japanese culture are unique. Japan's culture is different, of course, but customs change as social organization changes, and each generation may have different customs. That is why we cannot assume that culture is the same as social customs.

It is often said that the Japanese market is unique. But in fact, it is just the matter of consumer's priority. A Japanese customers look first at quality, while an Americans look first at the price tag. I believe that this is the real difference between Japanese and American consumers.

How Japan's Market Can Become More Vitalized

During and after World War II, Japan invested heavily in high-growth sectors. Times have changed since then, and if the Japanese people are to adapt to these changes they must find new ways to invest. First of all, any company that is active in an industry protected by government regulations will never become internationally competitive. Secondly, Japanese people must reconsider where they should invest their money and deposit their savings.

Japan should invest in sectors which have a potential for future growth, rather than depending on regulations and trying to bring back former conditions. The pouring of public funds into some of the nation's banks is a case in point. Investing money and human resources in a sector that is in decline, in an attempt to prop it up, will only lead to long-term decline.

Consumers are changing. First of all, they want new things, and to them "new" has a shorter life span than it used to. This means that styles which embrace change will stay in fashion, while things that try to maintain the *status quo* will disappear. Secondly, convenience stores, supermarkets, discount stores, catalog shopping and the Internet are giving consumers more opportunities to choose where to shop. Consumers are now willing to spend only on services and goods they need, so anyone who tries to sell things without understanding this market will not stay in business for long.

We can expect further developments in catalog shopping, and greater interest in amenities for the housing industry. For example, the shape and style of a bathroom or toilet used to be delegated to the builder, according to budget, but today's consumers specify the design, color and fixtures. The Japanese are going to show rooms, and consumer items boasting new designs and concepts are receiving a great deal of attention.

Japanese people are good at catching up to others, and by looking for ideas. And if they think they have gotten ahead, they look around to see if there are other ideas to adopt. For their part, American companies used to made efforts to catch up with Japan's production technology, introducing just-in-time delivery and other Japanese methods. In this way, each nation stimulates the other to further effort, and this adds energy to each market. More foreign investment in Japan would surely bring greater vitality to the Japanese market.

Japan — Cultural Change and Social Harmony

I like Japanese culture because it has so many different facets. As I mentioned a moment ago, we cannot say that culture is the same as social custom. Culture and customs both change, though customs change faster. Basic values do not change, I suppose, but they were surely not exactly the same in a feudal society as they are in an industrial society, and the values held by an industrial society are somewhat different from those in an information society. And even in the case of free economies existing in the same time span, basic values in London, for example, will be different from those in New York, and of course different again from those in Tokyo. Times and systems may change, but one thing that never changes is the desire for balanced harmony, for what the Japanese call *wa*.

People in Japan have recently begun showing a desire to express their own individuality and assert themselves. Some Japanese people worry that this tendency will undermine social equilibrium. But individuality and social harmony are not opposed to each other. After all, everyone knows that any expression of one's individuality must obey certain social rules. Company employees love Tora-san, the hero in the film series, because they are attracted to the way he showed the depths of his own personality. Yet Tora-san never tried to overturn social convention. He won the admiration of Japanese company employees who are continually forced to respect the position of others and who must stifle their own personalities.

I hope that the Japanese will find ways to maintain social harmony while letting each person be themselves, and that their contacts with the outside world will benefit from the self-confidence they will feel as a result.

GEORGE FIELDS

George Fields was born in Japan in 1928. He is an Australian citizen, and graduated with honors from the University of Sydney. He is fluent in English and Japanese, and has published in both languages. He founded ASI Market Research Japan, and served as its Chairman and CEO until 1993. He is President of Fields Associates, and occupies the position of Professor of Marketing at the Graduate School of Management and Information, Sanno College. He is also an adjudicator for "Best Corporate Leader and Organization," Toyo Keizai.

FOOD

The words "Japanese food" are likely to call to mind *sushi*, *tempura* or *suki-yaki*. Yet Japan's everyday cuisine has a far wider range.

Meals in Japan can be broadly divided into three types — Japanese, Western and Chinese — providing a great variety of menus to enjoy. In addition, magazines dedicated to culinary pleasures often introduce recipes from other Asian countries, Latin America, and elsewhere, allowing ingredients and preparation styles from all over the world to be adapted into Japan's culinary culture. Social trends, such as later marriages and more women entering the workforce, are changing eating habits.

People are dining out more at family restaurants and fast food outlets, and when they do eat at home they may choose instant or frozen foods that need little preparation time. With convenience stores open until late at night, more people are buying and eating food when it suits them, regardless of the hour.

Modern preservation techniques, and imported foods from countries with climates different from Japan's, have made it possible to buy almost any type of food at practically any time of year. Even so, the Japanese penchant for eating fresh foods in season still remains, and the desire to mark special events with food representing that time of the year still holds strong.

Breakdown of Average Monthly Living Expenditures per Household (All Household Base)

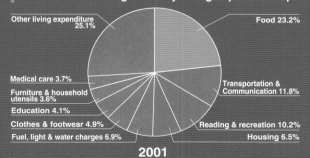

Other living expenditure 25.1%

Food 23.2%

Medical care 3.7%

Furniture & household utensils 3.6%

Education 4.1%

Transportation & Communication 11.8%

Clothes & footwear 4.9%

Fuel, light & water charges 6.9%

Reading & recreation 10.2%

Housing 6.5%

2001

Source: "Monthly Statistics of Japan", Statistics Bureau, Ministry of Public Management, Home Affairs, Post and Telecommunications

Change of Average Monthly Expenditures for Food and Share in Living Expenditures per Household

	¥	%
1997	78,306	23.5
1998	78,156	24.2
1999	76,590	23.7
2000	73,844	23.3
2001	71,534	23.2

Daily Meals

Despite Youth's Preference for Western Food, Rice Remains a Staple

The daily meal is usually based on a Japanese, Western or Chinese menu, with the latter two adapted, more or less, to Japanese tastes. Rice is the staple food. When Chinese side dishes are served, they come with rice, and this is often true with Western side dishes as well. To the Japanese, rice goes down best with a bowl of *miso* soup. *Miso* soup differs in tastes and ingredients, depending on the region and the home, thus typifying "Mom's" home cooking. The daily special at a restaurant will have a main dish and the inevitable rice and *miso* soup.

Bread is popular too, especially among women. More bakeries are selling freshly baked bread on counters open to the street, and some stores use recipes from a number of different countries. Bread is generally thought of as part of a light meal, so it is often eaten at breakfast, during a quick lunch, or as a snack.

Children prefer spaghetti (Italian), hamburgers (American), *ramen* noodles (Chinese), fried rice wrapped in a paper-thin omelet (a Western adaptation), and curried rice (an adaptation from India). The younger the child, the more likely they are to prefer Western food. This might indicate a slow drifting away from Japanese cuisine in Japan.

1. A typical western-style breakfast.
2. A typical breakfast served in the Japanese style.
3. In Japan, the four most popular Chinese dishes are *ramen* (noodles in broth), *gyoza* (stuffing in a pasta shell), *chahan* (fried rice with chopped delicacies), and *mabo-dofu* (tofu in a sauce).
4. Almost all kids like *omuraisu* (fried rice wrapped in a paper-thin omelet).
5. Spaghetti and other Italian dishes are growing in popularity in Japan.
6. *Suki-yaki* used to be considered a luxury dish.
7. *Sashimi* (raw, fresh seafood) tastes best after it is dipped in soy sauce.
8. *Tonkatsu* is eaten by all age groups. Some people say it gives extra stamina.
9. Cheap imported beef has made steak affordable for the Japanese.
10. Curried rice is one of the most popular meals in Japan.

At the Table

Lifestyle and Schedule Changes Affect Eating at Home

Some families eat the traditional way, sitting on *tatami* mats at a low table, while others eat Western style, on chairs at a table that is high by comparison.

To save money, a growing number of families will go to large discount outlets in the suburbs to buy liberal quantities of instant, canned and frozen foods, which have a long storage life. To satisfy the family's need for and love of fresh foods, housewives often go to a local supermarket or shop specializing in some delicacy.

Breakfast is served in one of two styles – Japanese or Western (see previous page).

Lunch for school children might be prepared by the school, or it could be brought from home or bought at a convenience store or store selling hot box lunches. Workers often bring a lunch from home, or eat out.

The evening meal is more elaborate in size and variety, and the ideal is for all family members to eat together. However, in today's busy world it is all too common for family members with conflicting schedules to eat different meals at different times.

1. Eating the traditional Japanese way.
2. In this noodle restaurant, customers eat standing up. Ideal for the busy businessperson who has only a few minutes before taking a train or getting back to work.
3. Sushi in this restaurant passes by on a "conveyor belt." This *kaiten* (revolving) *zushi* system makes for a somewhat untraditional *sushi* experience. The bill is calculated by counting up the number of plates you took.
4. In some residential districts you can buy vegetables at roadside stalls.
5. Beverages on display at a supermarket.
6. This market specializes in fresh seafood. The fish can be prepared the way you want it.
7. Beverage vending machines can be found at all kinds of places in Japan.
8. Western-style meals are also very popular.
9. Female office workers enjoying their lunch in a park.

Seasonal Dishes for Spring

Warm Sunshine, Colorful Food

When winter fades away and spring arrives, it's time to enjoy the sunshine, perhaps with a lunch outdoors. When the cherry blossoms throughout the country are in their prime, they seem to invite us to party under them. At this time of the year, the hues of spring are reflected in the colorful meals. The traditional box lunch for such an occasion comes in a number of varieties, including *chirashi-zushi* (colorful ingredients scattered on *sushi* rice). Exotic additions, like *nanohana* (rape blossoms), *taranome* (angelica buds) and *nemitsuba* (a type of honeywort), signify spring and are especially delicious.

1. *Chirashi-zushi* (foreground) is a feast for the eyes as well as the palate. Also shown: *momo no sekku* food for the Doll's Festival on March 3.
2. Japanese green tea and *o-hagi* rice dumplings covered with sweet bean paste.
3. *Sakura-mochi* rice cakes to celebrate spring. Japanese sweet foods use different shapes, colors and tastes to remind us of the current season.
4. *Takenoko* (bamboo shoots) appear only in the spring.
5. A lunch box for an outing in spring.
6. A Family enjoying a picnic.

Seasonal Dishes for Summer

Noodles Provide Refreshing Relief When Appetites Decline in the Heat

Summer in Japan means hot and humid weather. Appetites decline and some people lose weight. To forget the heat, we eat chilled noodles, perhaps thin ones (*somen*) in a light broth, or brown ones made of buckwheat (*soba*), or others served Chinese-style. A different approach might be to restore energy with some barbecued meat, *tempura* (deep fried delicacies), eel or a curried dish.

Summer also means a cold beer. Drop into a beer hall on the way home from work and you will surely find many businesspeople with the same idea. Stores also do a thriving business selling ice cream, ice candy and soft drinks.

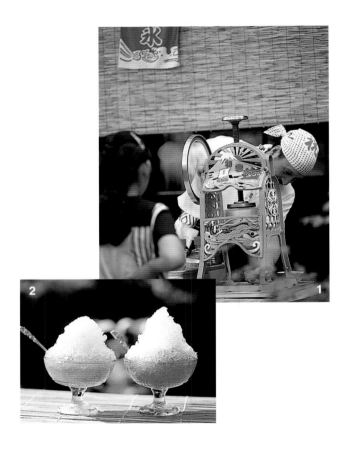

5

6

1. Making *kaki-kori*.
2. To make *kaki-kori*, just pour sweet syrup on finely sliced pieces of ice.
3. Fresh green soybeans go well with beer.
4. *Una-ju* (broiled eel on rice) is served on the Day of the Ox (July 20). People say it gives the energy we need to endure hot muggy days.
5. *Somen* (fine noodles served chilled in a light broth).
6. Chinese-style noodles served chilled. An excellent meal in the summer.
7. Chilled watermelon. Some people find it tastes even better with a sprinkling of salt.

Seasonal Dishes for Autumn

Fresh Food at Harvest Time

The fall months bring a lush harvest and revitalized appetites. Many fine foods are in season, adding special flavors to meals and announcing fall's arrival. This is a good time to eat rice cooked with freshly picked mushrooms, or Pacific saury with its appetizing fatty flavor. There is also fruit to enjoy, like apples and *nashi* pears.

1. Pacific saury is an autumn delicacy. To really enjoy it, broil it and eat with grated *daikon* radish and soy sauce.
2. Baked sweet potato.
3. Dried persimmons. In the old days, persimmons were often hung under the eaves to dry.
4. A family outing to pick *nashi* pears.
5. Kids always enjoy *o-nigiri* rice balls.
6. *Chuka-man* (Chinese-style steamed bun with special ingredients inside).
7. Rice boiled with chestnuts — a sign of autumn.

Seasonal Dishes for Winter

Warm Feelings and Hot Food Highlight Winter Celebrations

Christmas, New Year's Day, and parties before and after the New Year give us plenty of opportunity to have fun with people and celebrate.

Taking a page out of the West's cultural calendar, the Japanese have made Christmas Eve and Christmas Day a time to get together with friends and family, enjoying cake and eating good food. The cold weather outside tells us it's time for hot stews in a pot, or for *oden* (various simmered ingredients). Pot stews are fun to eat with family members and friends, so they are often seen at New Year's parties. On the last day of the year, it is customary to serve buckwheat noodles, as the long noodles represent the hope for a long life. The New Year brings us the traditional and colorful *o-sechi-ryori* cuisine and *o-zoni* (rice cakes in soup).

1. Christmas in Japan. Christmas cake is the star of the meal at this time of the year.
2. *Taiyaki* are fish-shaped pancakes. A sweet bean paste hides inside.
3. During the cold winter months, *sake* rice wine goes down well when heated.
4. This stall serves *oden* (various ingredients simmered in a pot).
5. *Kaki-nabe* (oyster in a pot). Oysters taste best in winter.
6. *Chanko-nabe* is a well known, high-calorie stew favored by sumo wrestlers.
7. *Yudofu* is an excellent way to enjoy *tofu* during the winter.

New Culinary Experiences

Authentic International Cuisine Adds Zest to Eating

Japan's Leisure Development Center claims in its *White Paper on Leisure* that eating out is the most popular leisure activity in Japan. Actually, eating out is gaining even more popularity. Magazines and TV programs specializing in culinary pleasures are enjoying a boom. Some authentic restaurants introduced in the media employ chefs from abroad — this way, patrons know they are eating the real thing. The media also promotes famous restaurants as interesting places for a date.

One overall trend is that Western food is growing in popularity. Italian restaurants, in particular, have enjoyed a boom that started around 1990. As you would imagine, their menus feature spaghetti and other pasta dishes, pizza, espresso and cappuccino coffee, *tiramisù*, *gelato*, and other items Japanese people will surely continue to enjoy.

Restaurants may present something other than the Japanese, Western and Chinese standbys. "Ethnic" restaurants have also appeared in urban areas, introducing food from many parts of the world.

Ingredients for foreign recipes are being imported in greater amounts and variety from all over the world, increasing opportunities to enjoy an international culinary experience.

1. Excellent restaurants serving cuisine from France, Italy and other nations have sprung up in cities, and are a popular destination for young couples on a date.
2. Gourmets have many magazines to choose from. Readers can find out about restaurants where the food is extra good.
3. Single people and working women find it convenient to buy prepared side dishes and eat them at home or at work.
4. A European-style streetside cafe.
5. Crepe are popular among the young.
6. Fast food is now popular in Japan, especially among the young.

Top Ten Food Imports for 2000

(US$1,000)

1. Pork, Porkscraps	3,253,854	6. Soybeans	1,229,388
2. Shrimp	3,042,075	7. Salmon, Trout	1,077,185
3. Beef	2,601,607	8. Wheat	1,034,597
4. Tuna, Bonito	2,121,280	9. Crab	992,209
5. Corn	1,888,567	10. Frozen vegetables	882,615

Source: Ministry of Finance

Change of Average Monthly Expenditures for Foods and Share of Expenditures for Restaurants in Total Foods per Household (All Household Base)

Source: Statistics Bureau, Ministry of Public Management, Home Affairs, Posts and Telecommunications

Trends in Eating and Drinking

Greater Variety in Food and Alcohol To Satisfy Individual Tastes

Against a backdrop of rising food imports from all over the world, the impression remains that Japanese food products are continuing to improve in quality. Food from certain parts of the country is particularly expensive, but is still much in demand because the place of origin has an excellent reputation — for example, *koshihikari* rice from Uonuma (Niigata Prefecture), mackerel from Seki, and beef from Matsuzaka. Organic vegetables also quickly find their way into shopping baskets, as interest in health food grows.

With more women in the workforce and later marriages, there is a strong demand for instant and frozen foods, side dishes partially prepared for eating at home, and ready-to-eat food and box lunches from convenience stores. These products have found a ready market among single people who have little time or inclination to stay long in the kitchen.

Beer is Japan's most popular alcohol. During FY 1998, each adult consumed an average of 63 liters of beer, about six times the amount of *sake* imbibed during the same period. Some domestic beer breweries are taking steps to make their operations environmentally friendly, by developing production methods which yield no garbage, using recycled materials for containers, and installing refrigeration equipment that is freon-free.

Demand for wine has blossomed since 1992, and imports continue to grow. In addition to products from countries which have exported wine to Japan for many years, wines from eastern Europe, South America and elsewhere are also enjoying growing attention.

1. Wine is said to have health-giving qualities, so has enjoyed a boom for some time. Wine imports from many countries are growing steadily.
2. Businesspeople like nutritional tonic beverages. Deregulation of the market has made it possible for convenience stores to sell them.
3. Mineral water comes in many brands, some imported, some domestic.
4. Instant meals, almost all featuring noodles, are cheap and easy to prepare. A favorite among single people and students.
5. Lunch-boxes at a convenience store. The store clerk will be glad to heat one up in a microwave for you.
6. With items like sparkling malt liquor (containing less than 66.7% malt) and imported beer now available, the alcohol market offers consumers a wide choice.

Imported and Domestic Wine Shipments

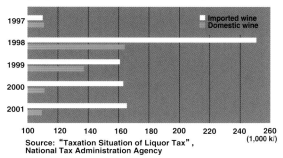

Source: "Taxation Situation of Liquor Tax",
National Tax Administration Agency

Mineral Water Imports

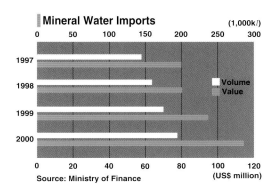

(1,000kℓ)

Source: Ministry of Finance

4

5

6

Traditional Dishes

Bountiful Nature Offers All Kinds of Seasonal Delicacies from Sea and Mountain

Food tastes best just after the harvest, as anyone who partakes of Japanese cuisine knows. Seafood and food from deep in the country is called "joys from sea and mountain," as a way of thanking nature for her bountiful supply of food.

The Japanese did not eat beef or pork before the Meiji Period, which began in 1868. Prior to that time, most animal protein came from seafood. It is therefore natural that different ways of preserving and serving seafood developed throughout Japan. One traditional menu is *sashimi*, a superlative way to eat fresh, raw fish.

What would Japanese cuisine be without rice? Boiled rice has been a staple food since ancient times. Cooked rice can also be pounded to make *mochi* rice cakes, and rice flour can be made into confectioneries. *Sake*, of course, is traditional rice wine. (See the article on rice and *sake*.)

Two of the most commonly used seasonings are soy sauce and *miso*. Both are made primarily from soy beans, which are rich in protein. Soy sauce is very versatile — it can be added to the ingredients when they are simmered or broiled, it can be sprinkled on food during the meal, or food can be dipped in it to pick up extra flavor. *Miso* has excellent nutritional and preservative qualities, and is found in many different recipes. Taste and color vary greatly by region — some *miso* are a reddish brown, some a very light color.

1

3

2

1. Meals celebrating the New Year contain ingredients that symbolize everyone's desire for good health and a long life.
2. *Nigiri-zushi* tastes best when dipped in soy sauce. This type of *sushi* has ancient roots.
3. Making pickles.
4. Steamed glutinous rice is pounded to make *mochi* rice cakes.
5. *Mochi* rice cakes are arranged to make a *kagami-mochi* decoration for the New Year.
6. On January 11, in a tradition called *kagami-biraki*, the *kagami-mochi* are cut, cooked and eaten in a sweet adzuki bean soup.
7. *Tempura*, one of Japan's most popular traditional dishes, features deep-fried fresh vegetables and seafood.
8. Buckwheat flour dough is kneaded, then cut into *soba* noodles.
9. To enjoy *zaru-soba* (buckwheat noodles served cold on a bamboo drainer), first dip the noodles in a sauce.

Rice and *sake*

The cultivation of rice began over 2,000 years ago in Japan. Since that time, the cycle of rice production, from spring sowing to transplanting in paddies to harvesting in autumn, has been repeated year after year. Because the rice harvest is largely dependent on the weather, a number of ceremonies offering prayers to the gods

Rice

have developed over the years. Japan has numerous festivals, many of them closely connected to agriculture, such as the Festival of Prayers for a Good Crop, and the Harvest Thanksgiving Festival. The earnest desire for a bumper crop reflects the fact that Japan has, through part of its history, not always been able to produce enough rice to feed its large population, although this is not a problem today.

Rice contains plenty of carbohydrate and protein, and typically serves as a staple food eaten with side dishes of fish and vegetables. It may be boiled and steamed to produce plain white rice, or boiled with adzuki beans to make *sekihan* (red rice, often eaten to celebrate some event), or boiled with seasonal vegetables to make *taki-komi gohan* (a rice dish that takes on the taste and color of the vegetables it is boiled with). A glutinous type of rice is steamed and pounded to make *mochi* (rice cakes).

As well as being the staple food, rice is also the basic ingredient of *sake* and a variety of vinegar. Japanese *sake* has the highest alcohol content of any brewed liquor.

Sake is made from a polished rice which, compared to ordinary rice, is less glutinous, has larger grains, and has more white core nutrients. Polished rice is made by removing the outer layers. The quality of the *sake* is said to depend partly on the percentage of white core nutrients remaining in the rice from which it is made. The smaller the core remaining, the better the *sake*. For instance, rice grains for eating have 91% of their core remaining (i.e., they are 9% polished). For ordinary *sake*, 60 - 70% of the rice remains after polishing, while for *ginjo-shu sake* less than 60% remains. In the case of *daiginjo-shu sake* , less than 50% remains.

Making one variety of *sake*, *ginjo-shu*, is considered to be the ultimate test of a brewer. It was made by brewers as a way of honing their skills. This type of *sake* has been on the market for only about ten years; prior to that, it was something of a secret and not available to anyone outside the trade.

Rice that will be made into *sake* is polished, then left to sit for about a month. It is then washed, and set aside for another day. Next, it is steamed. Then it is cooled to the appropriate temperature for the *koji* yeast, which will be used to ferment the mixture to produce an unpressed *sake* called *moromi* (main mash). Cooling in frigid air is said to produce the best *sake*. This excellent variety, called *kan-zukuri*, is brewed during winter.

The next step is to sprinkle *koji* yeast on the steamed rice (see photograph of worker). In traditional *sake*-making, this process lasts for two days and nights. During this time dedicated workers have practically no time to eat or sleep.

Next comes the making of the *moto*. This step is indispensable to making a pure yeast. The yeast is then mixed with water, steamed rice, and *koji* to allow the yeast cells to convert the rice starch into sugar. The action of the yeast produces alcohol, and the resulting *moromi* becomes unpressed *sake*. This process takes 20

Malted rice, yeast (*koji*) and water are mixed together to make *sake*.

Making Process

Rice
↓
Polished Rice
↓
Washed Rice
↓
Steamed Rice
↓
Moto (Speed Mash) ← Koji
↓
Water for Fermentation → *Moromi* (Main Mash)
↓
Pressurization & Filtration
↓
Fresh *Sake*
↓
Storage

to 30 days for ordinary *sake*, although for *daiginjo-shu* the *moromi* will be left to ferment for 35 to 45 days.

Finally, the *moromi* is pressed to remove the *sake* lees. The resulting liquid is then filtered to produce pure *sake*. Products other than the pure *sake* are sterilized by heating gently at about 60° Celsius, then allowed to mature in storage.

These days, the brewing process is mechanized and is done all year round. However, some brewers still produce *sake* in the traditional manner, at the most suitable time of the year.

In traditional *sake*-making, the chief brewer in charge of the process described above is called the *toji*. He is like an orchestra conductor — he must have a thorough understanding of the various processes involved, and must be able to guide his workers, showing them how to produce the perfect balance of flavor and aroma. The old proverb, "Teamwork makes good *sake*," underlies the importance of working together to achieve a common goal.

It is generally said that the quality of *sake* depends on the purity of the water. The exquisitely delicate yet pronounced taste of *sake* is the product of clear water, bountiful nature, and years of technical experience, not to mention the affection with which Japanese people regard rice.

Interior of a *sake* brewery

HOUSING

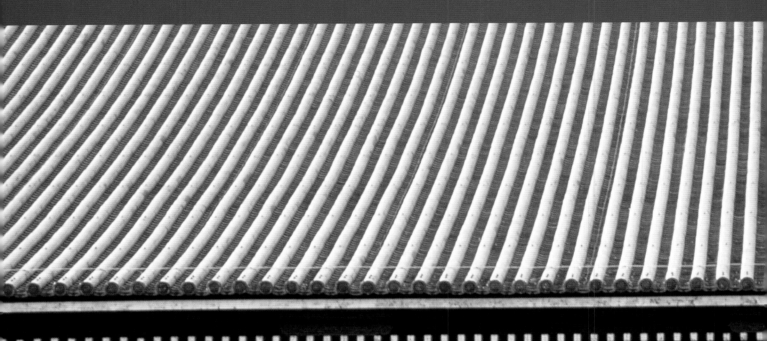

More than half of Japan is steep mountain or deep forest that is unsuitable for habitation. The cities are located in the plains, which occupy only a small part of the country. Housing conditions in these urban areas, where the population continues to grow, are far from ideal.

Dependence on public transport in large, crowded cities means that the housing environment itself is different from that in rural cities and the country. In the big city, people board trains and buses, so they want to live close to a station. Real estate agents advertising a house or apartment are sure to mention how many minutes it takes to walk to the nearest station. Land prices have declined somewhat since Japan's economic bubble burst, but the average company employee who wants to remain in the city still finds that a single dwelling of adequate size is beyond his reach.

Rural residents enjoy a better housing environment. They probably own a car, so they have greater choice of location. Their lots are larger, too.

Today's houses and lifestyles tend to take on a Western flavor. Even so, before entering the home everyone still takes off their shoes in the small vestibule. And some people, especially the elderly, still prefer a traditional room with its comfortable *tatami* mats.

One challenge facing housing in the future is that it must adapt to the needs of a population which is aging. To make it easier to look after elderly parents, families may want a home designed for two households, or a "barrier-free" home . Some people need an elevator in their home.

▌Breakdown of Average Monthly Living Expenditures per Household (All Household Base)

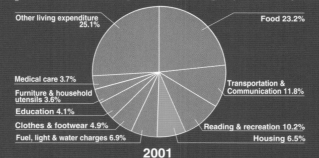

Other living expenditure 25.1%

Food 23.2%

Medical care 3.7%

Furniture & household utensils 3.6%

Education 4.1%

Clothes & footwear 4.9%

Fuel, light & water charges 6.9%

Transportation & Communication 11.8%

Reading & recreation 10.2%

Housing 6.5%

2001

Change of Average Monthly Expenditures for Housing and Share in Living Expenditures per Household

	¥	%
1997	22,308	6.7
1998	20,392	6.2
1999	21,041	6.5
2000	20,787	6.6
2001	20,018	6.5

Source: "Monthly Statistics of Japan", Statistics Bureau, Ministry of Public Management, Home Affairs, Post and Telecommunications

Modern Exteriors

Single Dwellings and High Rises — Individuality with a Western Flavor

Few single dwellings built today are designed to look like truly "Japanese" on the outside. Exteriors tend to draw inspiration from the West, or to combine Western and Japanese elements. Rural homes, such as those in farming villages, are the exception — there you will likely see that even new homes have a distinctive Japanese look. More and more, house structure is changing too, from wooden supports to reinforced concrete. Wood may be used on the facade to add a natural, warm touch.

Bed-towns in the suburbs are designed around a station and its neighboring stores. Further away, you will find single dwellings, large housing complexes, and condominiums.

Housing development projects in the past generally produced uniform apartment blocks, but the design of today's housing complexes respects the human need for varied lifestyles and individual sensibilities.

1. Single dwellings are built very close together in the suburbs of Tokyo.
2. A typical Japanese house built in the traditional style. The roof is covered with tiles, and the rooms and garden are comparatively spacious. This type of home is often seen in rural areas.
3. A two-story Western-style house with space for parking. This architectural style is common in the suburbs. This type of home is often seen in densely populated areas, where small, efficiently designed rooms are needed to make good use of limited space.
4. High rise apartment blocks. Standardized housing development projects were common in the past.
5. High rise living today emphasizes individuality. Condominiums and apartment buildings are built close to a station or bus route.
6. The Tama New Town housing development in Tokyo created Japan's first large bed-town.

Modern Interiors

Western Living Tempered with Traditional Lifestyles

Today's homes tend to combine two worlds — some rooms are in the Japanese style, others in the Western. Modern homes, whether single dwellings or condominiums, generally have more rooms designed in the Western style. The kitchen and children's rooms will almost always have a distinctively Western flavor. (With birthrates declining, children are probably lucky enough to have their own room.)

Any home with more than a minimum number of rooms will surely have at least one room designed in the traditional manner. Elderly people, especially, prefer the comfort of a Japanese room with its *tatami* mats.

If a bedroom has *tatami* mats, *futon* are taken out of the closet and laid on the floor for sleeping. A bedroom without *tatami* mats will have a bed.

Air conditioners which serve as heat pumps in the winter are common now, but when cold weather comes families will probably also use a *kotatsu* (a low table with an electric heater attached). The *kotatsu*, with its coverlet, is an inviting place for chatting and eating.

Changes in Average Floor Areas of Newly-constructed Housing

(m²/house)

	1997	1998	1999	2000	2001
Average	93.1	93.3	97.1	97.3	93.6
Privately owned houses	139.5	138.9	139.3	139.6	137.2
Houses for rent	52.5	51.4	52.3	53.5	51.9
Subsidized houses	71.9	75.1	69.7	70.4	72.2
Houses built for sale	92.7	92.4	94.6	96.6	98.2

Source: Ministry of Land, Infrastructure and Transport

5

6

4

1. A Japanese-style room with *tatami* mats and *shoji* doors and window coverings. To keep cozy in winter, people sit with their legs under a *kotatsu* (low table with an electric heater attached underneath).
2. Western-style kitchen.
3. Western-style dining-kitchen arrangement.
4. Western-style living room.
5. A study.
6. Bedroom for a child. In a country with low birth rates, children are likely to have their own bedroom, complete with key for extra privacy.
7. Japanese-style living room. *Zabuton* cushions on the *tatami* mats make sitting comfortable. The aesthetic effect is completed with the *kakejiku* (hanging scroll), *tokonoma* (alcove), and *chigai-dana* (staggered shelves) in the background.
8. A *genkan* (vestibule). Be sure to remove your shoes here before entering the home.

7

8

Trends in Housing

Homes — Reflecting the Individual Lifestyles of Young and Old

Mass-designed homes are not necessarily the norm now, since they do not fully respect individual lifestyle preferences. A growing number of prospective owners have a say in the design of their future single dwelling.

"Imported housing" (foreign houses and housing materials, particularly those exported from developed countries in Europe, North America and Oceania) experienced a temporary boom at one time and still enjoy considerable attention. As a result, the housing market now offers many foreign architectural styles and a greater amount and variety of materials and furniture, widening the options for both manufacturers and consumers. Imported products are bought not only for family dwellings but for second homes as well. Log houses are also popular among some people who buy them as their second home.

The housing environment is becoming more friendly for elderly and disabled people. For example: in certain cases toilets and baths are equipped with special devices to make caring for the disabled easier; some homes are designed to be "barrier-free," and elevators are being installed in some private homes.

As Japan's population ages, homes called *nisetai jutaku*, which are designed for two households living in the same dwelling, are increasing in number. Houses long ago were large and could accommodate three of more generations. Today's *nisetai jutaku* respect privacy more, since they are really two separate homes under one roof. Such houses are becoming more popular because, unlike in the U.S. and other developed countries, residential facilities for seniors are few in number and can therefore accommodate only a small percentage of elderly people in Japan.

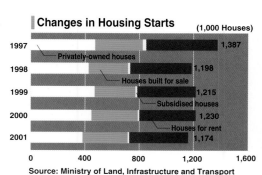

Changes of Number for Imported Houses

(Houses)

Types	FY1996	FY1997	FY1998	FY1999	FY2000
Log houses	281	424	565	1,078	795
2×4 types	4,456	5,152	5,199	6,447	5,182
2×4 panelized types	2,030	885	401	737	753
Post & beam types	97	94	130	257	116
Others	1,309	1,293	1,220	1,639	1,990
Total	8,173	7,848	7,515	10,158	8,836

Source: Questionnaire surveys of domestic companies that handle imported housing conducted by the Ministry of Land, Infrastructure and Transport, METI, the Japan 2×4 Home Builders' Association, and JETRO

Changes in Housing Starts

(1,000 Houses)

Privately-owned houses
Houses built for sale
Subsidised houses
Houses for rent

Year	Total
1997	1,387
1998	1,198
1999	1,215
2000	1,230
2001	1,174

0   400   800   1,200   1,600

Source: Ministry of Land, Infrastructure and Transport

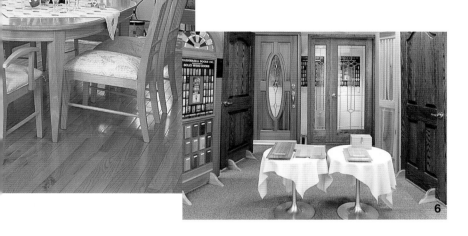

1. Apartment building constructed in the North American style.
2. Interior of a Western-style house made with imported materials. The furnishings are also imported, to maintain the same style.
3. Log houses are popular as cottages in highland resorts.
4. This room combines traditional Japanese sensibilities with a modern touch.
5. A modern home often has some Japanese style rooms, and others following a Western design.
6. Jetro Imported Housing Materials Center.
7. This bathroom makes it easier to care for elderly and disabled people.
8. A showroom displaying toilets for the elderly and disabled.
9. Manufacturers are developing motor vehicles to suit the needs of the disabled.

Traditional Exteriors

Natural Materials Offer Beauty and Simplicity

Although some regional variations exist, homes built in the traditional style tend to have wooden supports. Generally, such houses are faced with wood or clay, and roofed with tiles or, in a few cases, thatch. Bamboo hedges, or fences made of interwoven bamboo, may be seen around the house.

Japanese traditional businesses and restaurants often hang a *noren*, or split curtain, outside. The *noren* tells customers that the store or restaurant is open for business. It probably displays the name of the business or the owner's family crest.

1. Old fashioned dwellings stand side by side to make an aesthetically interesting cityscape.
2. You may see thatched roofs in rural areas.
3. Traditional dwelling with storehouse (building in foreground).
4. Latticework for a traditional touch.
5. Storehouse window.
6. One design for storehouse walls is called *namako-kabe*. Raised plaster covers the gaps between the square tiles. (Cover photo)
7. Mill with water wheel. In the old days, grain was ground at mills like this one.
8. Walls built in the *azekura* style are composed of logs which have a triangular cross section. The interior of the storehouse remains at a fairly constant humidity, because of the ability of wood to shrink.

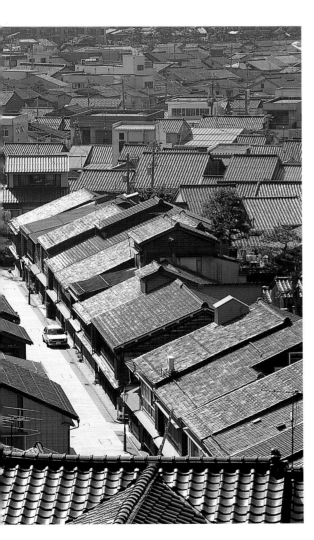

Traditional Interiors

Ingenious Techniques Added Comfort To Life in the Past

Wood, earth and paper are three materials used to advantage in the typical house of the past. The floors are covered in comfortable *tatami* mats. Rooms are separated from each other by *fusuma* or *shoji* sliding doors. Both types of doors are light frameworks of wood — *fusuma* are covered with opaque paper, *shoji* with a white paper that allows some light through but conceals the interior of the room. By removing the *fusuma*, we can join the rooms together to make a large interior space. And by leaving the large *fusuma* or *shoji* open, we let air pass through the house, cooling and ventilating it. House structure is thus quite different from that of other countries.

The traditional home will also have *sudare* screens suspended from the eaves. The screens are rolled down in the summer, to shut out the sun's hot glare while letting cool breezes in. The old-fashioned mosquito net, hung around and over the *futon* bedding at night, was similar in the sense that it let air in but kept the bugs out.

Ancient houses had an *irori* (sunken hearth), which was the focal point of the home. On cold days it was an excellent place to get warm and chat.

1. *Shoji* sliding doors have a thick paper glued to the wooden latticework.
2. Part of a Japanese garden. Here you can see a *tsukubai* (stone basin for washing hands), and *tobi-ishi* (stepping stones).
3. The *tsubo-niwa* is a tiny garden laid out so that it is practically part of the house.
4. Interior of a house built long ago. The *irori* (sunken hearth) shown in the left foreground was used for cooking and to keep warm in winter.
5. The *kamado* stove was used for cooking food in pots and cauldrons.
6. Sun shining gently through the *shoji* sliding door gives a Japanese touch.
7. Interior of a house built in the *gassho-zukuri* (steep rafter) style.
8. *Doma* (entranceway with an earthen floor). In some cases the earth would be covered with a layer of cement.
9. A *koshido* (lattice door) lets in light through the gaps in the small vertical and horizontal strips of wood.

The Traditional Japanese Room

Over the centuries, Japanese houses adapted to the country's hot, humid climate. Then, during the rapid economic growth in the 1960s, housing design changed significantly, with reinforced concrete construction becoming more common. Today, though, the Japanese are rediscovering the unique qualities and advantages of the traditional Japanese-style room.

Japan is hot and humid in summer, yet very dry in winter. According to the Japan Weather Association, the moisture content of one cubic meter of air in the Kanto (Tokyo) region varies from 3 grams in winter to 15 grams in summer. By way of comparison, moisture content in the Middle East (for example, Iran) is 6 to 8 grams all year round. On this scale, then, Japan in winter is generally much drier than the Middle East, with about half the moisture content.

Furthermore, summer moisture content in Japan is a staggering five times higher than in winter. Traditional Japanese architecture mitigates the effects of this difference. During the humid summer, moisture is absorbed into the earthen walls, the *washi* (paper) sliding doors, and the *tatami* mats of straw and rush. During the dry winter, this moisture is gradually released into the room. In this way, traditional building materials help to maintain a year-round environment that is both healthy and comfortable.

These traditional materials also offer a potential solution to the increasingly worrisome problem of indoor atmospheric pollution, caused by harmful substances in modern construction materials, such as the glue used in plastic wallpaper. The traditional home is an extremely healthy environment — all of the components, including *tatami* mats, *washi* paper, earthen walls, and wooden supports, are made from natural materials. *Tatami* mats and *washi* sliding doors are particularly good at absorbing harmful substances. And when the house has ended its useful life, all of the materials can be disposed of or burnt safely, without producing any harmful by-products. *Washi* paper is very environmentally friendly— it is made not from trees but from paper mulberry and *mitsumata* plants, which can be harvested every year. There are attempts to reuse *washi* as fertilizer.

The Japanese room offers not only functional advantages but aesthetic beauty as well. For instance, the *washi* paper glued on sliding doors can give quite different results, depending on texture, color, and thickness. The grainy texture of the paper can be employed to deliberately accentuate the joins. Similarly, one can achieve a very different effect by applying glue to the entire paper surface, or by applying it just to the edges. When used on sliding doors or as wallpaper, *washi* can create a wide range of designs. It also ages gracefully, unlike

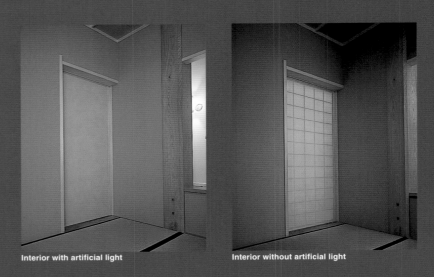

Interior with artificial light   Interior without artificial light

A Japanese-style room

plastic wallpaper, which looks good at first but soon takes on a grimy appearance. The subtle aging process of *washi* over time is fascinating to observe.

Another charm of the traditional room is the effect of light and shade. The shadows created by sunlight filtering through paper screens, and the light and shadows of flickering candles, were considered an important aesthetic element of the home. As homes adopted fluorescent lighting during the period of rapid economic growth in the 1960s, the beauty of shadows all but disappeared from Japanese homes. The soft light of the *andon* (a lamp stand enclosed in *washi*) is beautiful, even when the light comes from an electric bulb, rather than a candle. More and more people, both in-

side and outside Japan, are now appreciating the special mood created by indirect lighting.

The traditional Japanese room is a flexible living space that can be partitioned with sliding doors as required. The room caresses its inhabitants with natural materials, soothing hues, and light and shade. The traditional values and aesthetic beauty of the Japanese room are surely treasures to pass on to future generations in the 21st century.

Regional Variations

Climatic Differences Mean Different Styles of Architecture and Living

Geography and topography have created a number of climate zones in Japan. North is different from south, and the Pacific seaboard experiences weather quite different from that of lands bordering the Sea of Japan. As a result, living and housing conditions vary, depending on region. For example, areas subject to heavy snowfall may have steep roofs, typified by the ancient *gassho-zukuri* style. In the south, people on Ishigaki Island built strong, tall stone walls around their homes to protect themselves from the numerous typhoons. Trading centers built beautiful warehouses, creating a distinctive cityscape.

Many of these architectural features have disappeared with the passage of time. Municipal governments have protected some that remain, partly as a way to attract tourists.

In rural areas, you can still see homes where three generations live together. As the family expands in time, another house (*hanare*) may be built on the same family lot.

1

1. *Gassho-zukuri* (steep rafter) houses were often built in areas where much snow fell in winter. Snow cannot accumulate much on such steep roofs.
2. The ridges between rice paddies make a great path for kids on their way home from elementary school.
3. In many residential areas, you can see traditional and modern architectural styles side by side.
4. Interior of a *gassho-zukuri* house.
5. Getting heavy snow off the roof.
6. Houses on Ishigaki Island in Okinawa Prefecture. The strong stone walls around homes give some protection from typhoons.
7. Evening in a farming village.

2

Japanese Gardens through the Seasons

SPRING

Taizo-in Temple (Kyoto Prefecture)

SUMMER

Ritsurin Park (Kagawa Prefecture)

FALL

Tenjuan Garden (Kyoto Prefecture)

WINTER

Kenrokuen Garden (Ishikawa Prefecture)

RECREATION

Company employees are working fewer hours, and modern electric appliances have made household chores less time consuming. Little wonder, then, that the Japanese are now asking themselves how they can enjoy all that leisure time. Ambitions are changing too — people are less keen on living affluently and more interested in achieving quiet contentment. Disposable income, formerly dedicated to acquiring more things, is now being used for travel, leisure, and other activities that bring a sense of inner satisfaction.

Since the beginning of the 1990s, people tend to be more careful about expenditures on money. Outdoor activities for the entire family, which need not cost a lot, are enjoying a boom. Campgrounds and fishing spots accessible by car have become popular places for families and young adults. Campgrounds have sprung up all over the country, and outdoor goods and recreational vehicles are selling well.

Leisure in the home probably involves electronic media items. There are more TV channels to watch, which means more programs to record. CDs and MDs (mini disks) are two formats for the music lover. Then there are computer games for the entire family, and surfing the Net.

On weekends and holidays, people may stay home and watch TV, or eat out, or enjoy a day of shopping.

Breakdown of Average Monthly Living Expenditures per Household (All Household Base)

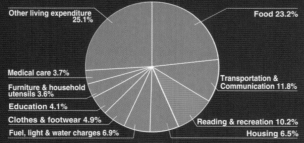

Other living expenditure 25.1%

Food 23.2%

Medical care 3.7%

Furniture & household utensils 3.6%

Education 4.1%

Clothes & footwear 4.9%

Fuel, light & water charges 6.9%

Transportation & Communication 11.8%

Reading & recreation 10.2%

Housing 6.5%

2001

Source: "Monthly Statistics of Japan", statistics Bureau, Ministry of Public Management, Home Affairs, Post and Telecommunications

Change of Average Monthly Expenditures for Reading & Recreation and Share in Living Expenditures per Household

	¥	%
1997	32,833	9.9
1998	32,434	9.9
1999	33,378	10.3
2000	32,126	10.1
2001	32,418	10.2

Leisure

Three Holiday Seasons for Travel and Homeward-Bound Trips

Answers to the question, "What is important in your life?", are now likely to be: enjoying natural surroundings, personal health, and family. Outdoor activities, like fishing or camping trips involving use of the family car, can satisfy all of these interests.

Getting away from it all is possible during Japan's three holiday seasons: New Year's, "Golden Week" (a string of holidays around the beginning of May), and O-Bon (summer holidays around August 15). The ideal trip within Japan is to some tourist spot, with night accommodations at a hot spring. Every part of the country has a popular spa.

Travelers going overseas now have a wide choice of destinations. They can join a conventional group tour, or design their own trip to almost any corner of the globe. Stay at homes have plenty of television channels to choose from, and more late night shows as well.

Amusement parks, zoos and leisure centers attract many families and young couples on their holidays. Theme parks carve out a niche for themselves by presenting some unique thematic attraction. They organize events for every season, and keep developing new ways to attract visitors.

1. Hiking is an excellent way to get close to nature.
2. On weekends and holidays, families flock to Ueno Zoo in Tokyo.
3. Domestic travelers are likely to have a hot spring as one of their destinations. Everyone likes to go to a spa for mental and physical relaxation. Well known hot springs are scattered all over the country.
4. Movie theaters continue to attract large crowds. Japanese animated films and Hollywood productions are especially popular.
5. Golf enthusiasts are generally above a certain age. Games are broadcast live on TV almost every week.
6. Fishing is a favorite sport for many people. Some go to the sea, others prefer rivers.
7. Mountain climbing.

Sports

Sports for Fun and Physical Fitness

Baseball is one of the most popular sports in Japan. Just about every school has a baseball club. Many adults join an amateur team that plays for their company or neighborhood. Sports enthusiasts participate in other games as well, like soccer (a game for the young), golf (for the middle aged), and gateball (for the elderly).

Sports are not only for playing. With more TV channels now on the air, there are plenty of chances to watch live professional baseball, J.League soccer, golf, and other sporting events. Important sports events in other countries are also broadcast live by satellite.

Multi-purpose stadiums are being built in many parts of Japan, making it easier to go and cheer on one's favorite professional team.

1. The national high school baseball championship games are an important part of summer entertainment. Baseball is Japan's most popular sport, both at the amateur and professional level.
2. Many people jog or join a fitness club to become physically fit.
3. Older adults like gateball, a game that evolved in Japan.
4. Sports clubs have sprung up in urban areas. Company employees drop in on their way home from the office.
5. Honing their swimming skills at a sports club. Quite a few swimmers are older adults.
6. Ever since J.League's inauguration, soccer has drawn huge crowds, especially young people.

Spring and Summer

The Mountains and Seashore Beckon on Hot, Muggy Days

Many company employees take their summer holidays in mid-August, during the O-Bon festivities. This is a good time to travel, perhaps to one's home town. Resorts attract families and others who want to get away from the heat. Other families and young adults also head for the outdoors.

Swimming in the sea and marine sports are very popular in July and the first half of August. Japan is surrounded by the ocean, but there are surprisingly few places where you can swim safely. So famous beaches are sure to be crowded when the swimming season is in full swing.

Large pools and water sports facilities in suburban areas offer plenty of attractions and are easy to get to by road or rail.

1. Running the rapids by kayak. Training sessions offer a chance to learn more about the sport.
2. Well-known beaches attract many families and the young crowd every fine day.
3. Campgrounds are a good place for family fun. More and more people are coming to campgrounds by car to enjoy the outdoors.
4. When the cherry trees bloom, it's time to come and enjoy the beauty of spring.

Fall and Winter

Sporting Events in Autumn, Skiing in Winter

Fall is generally the best time of the year for sports. This is when schools hold track and field days and athletic events, and when a wide variety of sports competitions are held for adult fans.

In warmer parts of the country, winter is a time for marathons and long relay races. Many other important sporting events are also held, most of them shown live on TV on a weekly basis.

Winter snows bring out the skis. The northern island of Hokkaido and the Tohoku and Shinshu regions of Honshu have many ski slopes which are easy to get to. Snowboarding has recently become as popular as skiing among the young crowd.

When schools and workplaces close down for the New Year's holidays, many people take off on a trip or go to their home towns, just as they do during the summer holidays.

5

6

1. Schools hold track and field days every fall.
2. Schools organize excursions in the fall. Everyone brings a box lunch and sets out for a tourist spot or place of interest.
3. Fishing with lures and imitation flies is a popular sport, among women as well.
4. Crystal clear water and autumn colors.
5. Winter means skiing. Ski slopes are now easy to get to, so day trips from metropolitan areas are possible.
6. Snowboarding is as popular as skiing among the young crowd.

Recreation Trends

Services Expand As Interest in Hobbies Grows

Well-established hobbies are evolving with the help of the latest technology. *Karaoke* is one example. When enjoying this "sing-along" hobby, enthusiasts read the lyrics on a screen linked to a computer — new networking technologies have made it possible to download more songs in a shorter time frame.

Magazines report future sales of music and video software, and give the latest details on leisure facilities and upcoming events. Some convenience stores have machines for placing orders for such items. Convenience stores are becoming increasingly important in the recreation scene, answering the needs of people near them.

Tending plants in small areas at home is another pastime that is growing in urban areas, especially among married women. Supplies and a wide variety of books catering to this hobby are sold at do-it-yourself stores and other outlets.

1. A good *pachinko* pin ball player can win many balls. The greater the number of balls, the better the prize. Games using LCD screens have recently gained much attention.
2. In a "karaoke box," amateurs sing to recorded instrumental music while reading the lyrics on the screen.
3. Magazines featuring travel and food are being published in increasing numbers, to satisfy demand as people find they have more spare time. Such magazines are sold in convenient stores and many other places.
4. More and more people, especially women, are trying to get close to nature in the big city by tending plants at home.
5. A flea market.
6. This store rents video cassettes. Watching movies at home is a favorite way to spend one's leisure hours. Some stores rent CDs.
7. A bowling alley. One recent innovation is computerized score keeping.
8. The Tokyo Imported Automobile Show. Foreign manufacturers are keen to make inroads in Japan by meeting the demands of the Japanese market - for example, installing the steering wheel on the right.

Leisure Activities Ranked by the Number of Participants (2001)

Rank	Leisure Activity	10,000 persons
1	Dining out (excluding daily meals)	7,800
2	Tourist travel within Japan	6,430
3	Driving	6,180
4	Karaoke	5,150
5	Video watching (including rental video)	4,740
6	Music listening (CDs, records, tapes, FM radio, etc.)	4,430
6	Zoos, botanical gardens, aquariums, museums	4,430
8	PCs (games, hobbies, communications, etc.)	4,140
9	Gardening	4,080
10	Movie (excluding television)	4,050

Source: Institute for Free Time Design

New Category Leisure Activities Ranked by Participating Ratio (2000)

Rank	Leisure Activity	Ratio (%)
1	Spa facilities (soaks in a spa)	36.9
2	Talking by cellular phones	29.7
3	Walking	26.1
4	Pet keeping	24.9
5	Raise and care of ornamental plants	22.8
6	Gardening	20.7
7	Home health exercise using instruments	19.5
8	Planning and participating to local festivals	15.2
9	Massage	10.7
10	Nature and street watching	9.8

Source: Institute for Free Time Design

Multimedia and Telecommunications

Mobile Communications and High-Tech Innovations Bring a New Dimension to Life

Telecommunication and networking developments have expanded communication possibilities for consumers. As but one example, more and more homes are being connected to the Internet.

Cellular phones, PHS mobile phones, and pocket pagers are ideal for business and private use, making it possible to get in touch with someone anytime, anywhere. Young people are also a receptive market for these items.

Computer games for the home and the arcade have seen impressive technical innovations. The result has been an ever-growing variety of games, some of which take you to a virtual world of action. "UFO Catcher" and *purikura* ("Print Club") machines provide something memorable to take home, and so are great hits among the young.

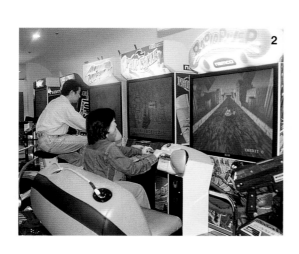

2

3

1. More and more people are using the Internet for their personal use. They find it a good way to satisfy their curiosity and send messages to friends.
2. Young people can feel like they are part of the action at a game center.
3. Here, families find it easy to decide what kind of game software they want.
4. At the Tokyo Game Show, families can sample computer games.
5. The *purikura* ("Print Club") machine takes a picture of friends or lovers, then prints it out in the form of small stickers.
6. *Purikura* stickers. Ideal for sticking in a notebook or on small objects.
7. Cellular and PHS phones are tremendously popular, and are used everywhere for business and personal use. Telecommunication companies compete with each other, offering ever more attractive prices and service.

Traditional Pastimes

Old Games and Artistic Disciplines Live On

Each period in Japanese history saw the development of various ways to pass the time. Ancient games still played to this day generally have some connection with annual events. For example, at New Year's the traditional family might play *fuku-warai* (blindfolded players add features to a face), *sugoroku* (a board game using dice), *hyakunin-isshu* (a poetry game), or *karuta* (a card game). Outdoors, old-fashioned kites are flown at the New Year.

Shogi is a board game something like chess. It is still quite popular, especially among older people. Some enthusiasts have even become professional players.

Shodo (calligraphy) students search for beauty through Chinese characters and Japanese letters. *Kado* or *ikebana* (flower arrangement) expresses the moods of the current season through flowers. These two arts attract many people, who continually strive to improve their skills while looking for a sense of inner peace. A growing number of people are taking up these traditions as hobbies.

1. *Hanafuda* cards have fanciful designs. They are used in a card game.
2. Kite flying in Japan takes on unique proportions.
3. A traditional *rakugo* performance. The narrator's mono-logues deal with comical social situations.
4. *Shogi* is somewhat similar to chess. The players tend to be above a certain age.
5. The game of *go* also tends to attract older people.
6. *Shodo* (calligraphy) involves the use of a brush and liquid ink. This ancient art requires skill and concentration.
7. *Ikebana* flower arrangements call to mind the current season. The idea is to achieve an overall aesthetic effect. *Ikebana* has many different artistic styles.

Japan —
A Blend of Changing Customs and Unchanging Values

We Japanese people have made life very easy for ourselves, but in doing so we have lost many intangible, yet valuable things. When I was a young girl, my mother used to make *o-inari-san* (rice in fried bean curd skins) for me to eat at lunch, whenever my school organized a field day or day trip. But today a mother will probably just pick up a box lunch for her child at a convenience store or supermarket. Many children today never experience that special feeling of warmth that I experienced because of my mother's extra care.

Our food is another case in point. Biotechnology and modern cultivation methods make it possible to buy many types of food at any time of the year. As a result, we have lost the enjoyment of savoring foods in season. This seasonal sensation was once considered important by the Japanese. We used to look forward to summer, or any season for that matter, because we could finally eat some special delicacy. Now we can shop by telephone or even computer — another modern convenience, but the down side is that we have less chance for human contact.

Mass production and mass consumption have brought us the throw-away society, which in turn has brought us monumental garbage problems. At the end of the Edo Period (1868), production was less than today, but people recycled everything. When a kimono was too old to wear, they cut it up and used it as rags. Even human excrement was valuable as fertilizer. These days, I feel the need to pass things on to the next generation, because once things are broken they disappear forever.

My Next Challenge — Working As a Goodwill Ambassador to the UNDP

I have just been to Cambodia for the first time, as a Goodwill Ambassador for the United Nations Development Program (UNDP). Actually, before the UN approached me I had never even heard of the program. So when I began preparing for the job I had to start from scratch. I don't have much experience because I am still comparatively young, and I don't know a great deal about politics or economics, but I think I can use my position as a novice to advantage. You see, my current situation places me in an excellent position to explain UNDP activities, and I will have a different point of view from which to explain the meaning of development assistance, 10 or 20 years from now. I realize my current shortcomings, so I won't rush into things — I'll start by just observing conditions when I get there.

I once visited India and Nepal as a television reporter. The job made me redefine my concept of affluence. People in developing countries are considered "behind the times" because they have less money and tend to live in smaller houses, compared to standards in industrialized countries. But the kids there do not know what being "behind the times" means, and they look at you with such happy, innocent faces. By comparison, Japanese kids seem weighed down, at a loss. In Japan, since in many cases both the father and mother work, they buy their children videos, computer games, and other things to take the place of their absent parents. As a result, Japanese children have no time to relax their minds by doing nothing. And when they play, they're probably just pushing buttons on some electronic device — they don't know how to be creative and make their own toys. If Indian or Nepalese children have nothing to play with, they'll probably draw something in the sand, and if they have only one toy, they'll take turns playing with it. They certainly know how to take good care of what they have. Japanese kids get whatever they want from their parents or grandparents, so they don't feel the need to look after things.

We Japanese are loosing touch with nature. Trees and green spaces are disappearing from our cities. We seldom get our shoes muddy! It was a shock to me when I walked along a muddy road with my son the first time — he hated it! Another time, he was so excited when he saw a common wood louse. He knew that the world has all kinds of insects, but he learned that from TV — he had little chance to experience such simple facts for himself. Japan has become affluent, and has an abundance of consumer goods, but are we wealthy in the true meaning of the word? I want my child to know that he and other Japanese children in our affluent society are actually the exception in this world.

The Changing Role of Japanese Women

We Japanese women have more choices than before. Japan's economic miracle has made it possible for married women to ask themselves, "Do I want to stay home and look after my family, or do I want to express myself by getting a job, or do I want to do both?" I know that I cannot do everything perfectly, so I want to do something which can only be done at a certain moment, and which has the greatest importance for that moment. Because of my son's age, I try to spend as much time with him as possible. It seems to me that if I really want to do something, I have to be prepared to sacrifice other things.

They say that women have finally achieved equality with men in Japan, but I don't agree. Women are still not viewed as equals, people expect a lot of women, and we certainly have to carry a heavy load. Of course, it is true that until the recent past Japanese women spent all their time doing the housework and looking after their children, whereas now we have the means and the time to dress up and become more cultured. Women in developing countries have to do the housework, raise their children, and do physical work outside the home as well. In some countries, their average life span is less than men's.

As I grow older, I want to learn more about Japan and Japanese culture. One day, I'd like to live a refined, traditional Japanese lifestyle. I want to become the kind of woman who looks stunning in a kimono. And when I meet foreigners, I'd like to show them the real Japan, so that they will appreciate Japanese women for their subtle refinements, their warmth, their empathy, and their concern for the well-being of others.

I love Japan, and am glad I was born here. When I go abroad, I want to do my best, and create a good impression of Japan.

MISAKO KONNO

Ms. Konno graduated from the Department of Literature at Keio University. She made her debut in 1979, and took the leading role in the NHK drama, *To Weave a Rainbow*, in 1980. She was awarded the Japan Academy Prize for supporting actress in 1987. She is active in movies and television, and on stage. She was named Goodwill Ambassador to the United Nations Development Program in October, 1998.

TV Asahi's *Misako Konno's House of Science* has run for almost 15 years. Her *The Flying Scallop*, a collection of scientific essays, won the Japan Literary Art Awards' women's literature prize. In February 1998, she appeared in a television program, *Misako Konno's Voyage of Discovery — Diary of India and Nepal*, to raise awareness of Japan's official development assistance.

Festivals and Ceremonies

Festivals that Hold Nature in Awe

Every month of the year, you can experience a large, traditional festival somewhere in Japan. Many festivals have some connection with agriculture, expressing the wish for a healthy crop in the spring, for freedom from pests and disaster in the summer, and for an excellent harvest in the fall.

Tremendous fireworks displays seem to be an essential part of summer in many parts of the country. When the sky lights up, you will see quite a few people dressed in cotton *yukata*, holding *uchiwa* fans.

1. Fireworks light up the summer sky all over Japan. One display may use up tens of thousands of fireworks.
2. *Umaoi* (driving horses) is an ancient tradition that requires the concentration of a samurai.
3. *Nodate* tea ceremonies are performed outdoors in the spring.
4. Children in festive dress.
5. *O-Bon* dances are held throughout Japan during the *Bon* festival, around August 15 each year.
6. During the Sanja Festival in Asakusa, Tokyo, men wear *happi* jackets and carry *o-mikoshi* portable shrines in a boisterous show of energy.

Martial Arts

Spiritual Growth — The Ultimate Purpose of Martial Arts

In ancient times, martial arts were practiced as part of samurai training. Today, though, their purpose is simply to develop physical agility and mental alertness. The emphasis is on respect and decorum. This may explain why some junior and senior high schools require that boys practice a martial art, such as judo or *kendo* (Japanese fencing), during part of the physical education curriculum.

1. Japanese archery (*kyudo*).
2. This building, called the Budokan, was built for the Tokyo Olympics (1964), and is now a popular spot for Japanese martial arts.
3. *Kendo* was first used to train men in the art of swordsmanship, during the time of the samurai.
4. Judo is practiced in many countries, and has become an Olympic sport.
5. Banners with the names of individual wrestlers decorate this sumo stadium.

Sumo Wrestling

KABUKI

Performance of a famous *kabuki* play called *Shibaraku*

Kabuki is one of the best forms of traditional entertainment for the ordinary citizen. People in the Edo period (1603-1868) had two places where they really wanted to pass the time — the sumo ring and the *kabuki* theater. Sumo wrestling still draws huge crowds, but *kabuki*, unfortunately, is not nearly as popular, because many Japanese mistakenly believe that *kabuki* is difficult to understand.

The attraction *kabuki* holds for everyday people is, first of all, the atmosphere of the theater. The play has already started, but we can enter and leave the theater whenever we like. Indeed, some people say it is good form to arrive a little late. Except at a few theaters,

there is nothing wrong with eating in the theater during the play. Drinking is fine too — even alcohol. While an actor is giving the performance of his life, someone may keep whispering to a friend, but this too is accepted. An enthusiastic fan might call out his appreciation to his favorite actor on the stage. Earphones are available for people from abroad and anyone else who wants to know exactly what is happening. The informal nature of *kabuki* sets it apart from the stiff atmosphere of a Western play or a concert of classical music.

Japanese people find many of the *kabuki* stories quite unrealistic, perhaps even absurd. One of the most absurd stories of all unfolds

The *Kabuki-za* Theater in Tokyo

in a scene called *Terakoya* (The Elementary School), in the play, *Sugawara Denju Tenarai Kagami*. To save the life of a feudal lord, a parent willingly lets a son die.

Although Japanese people can relate to the ancient ideal of serving one's feudal lord faithfully, they could never understand a parent treating a child as some material object to be sacrificed for a lord. Their modern democratic sentiments make such understanding impossible. Everyone in the audience realizes the absurdity of the scene. But the story is often told on the stage, and is always very well received.

The audience is more than willing to forget the absurdity and enjoy the action. "This could never happen," they think, "so let's just sit back and watch." The scene has depth — as the mother looks at the severed head of her son, the audience watches intently, waiting to see how the actor will play the role. There she is, controlling her unimaginable grief. It is the people in the audience who are crying. The scenario is absurd, but the audience is enthralled. They love the play.

When the curtain is drawn, everyone applauds loudly, glad they have come. Then, forgetting the heavy gloom of the play entirely, they eat the food they brought with them and go to the theater kiosk to see what's for sale.

In today's busy world there is little chance to enjoy a few leisurely hours at the theater. Even if you have the time, many other kinds of entertainment may entice you as well. But do go to a *kabuki* theater just once, to feel the atmosphere. You will enter a fascinating world that I know you will never forget.

Hinoemata *Kabuki*, a variety of *kabuki* developed in Fukushima Prefecture

Readers of this book are introduced to four facets of modern life in Japan — clothing, housing, food, and pastimes. Japanese lifestyles and consumer habits have certainly changed over the last 100 years, and they are continuing to change dramatically, as we can see in the recent evolution of the always-open convenience store, or the new passion for hobbies and leisure. The Economic Planning Agency has recently reported that consumers are turning their attention from spending on only material goods (clothing, housing and food) to attaining personal well-being. This new focus is seen in efforts to better oneself, to communicate more effectively with others, and to participate more actively in society.

Bettering oneself involves attempts to improve oneself physically, technically and mentally. This desire has resulted in a tendency to spend money on things that foster a more active life and a sense of personal well-being.

Consumer values change dramatically, and today's lifestyles embrace novelty and speed. But some things do not change. The ancient Japanese love of food and natural objects typifying the current season is one thing that remains constant. It is hoped that the reader will obtain a better understanding of the many aspects of life in Japan today.

This book has drawn on information found in various issues of *Japanese Market Report* and *Your Market in Japan* (available in English), which JETRO publishes to provide an overview of the Japanese Market, by item group.

With the Cooperation of:

Daiei Co., Ltd.

JETRO Housing Materials Center

Mitsukoshi

NAS (Nippon Aerobics Service)

NISSAN Motor Co., Ltd.

Showa Sangyo Co., Ltd.

TOTO Ltd.

Tokyo Fashion Week

Tokyo Imported Automobile Show

Tokyo Matsuya Co., Ltd.

Tokyu Home Corporation

TSUTAYA

Tetsuo UENO

JAPANESE LIFESTYLES

Published by:
Japan External Trade Organization (JETRO)
Information Services Department
2-5, Toranomon 2-chome, Minato-ku,
Tokyo 105-8466, Japan
Tel.03-3582-3518
http://books.jetro.go.jp

©JETRO 2002
First Edition, 1999
Sixth Printing, 2002
Second Edition, 2002